Edward Moseman,

a gift from the authors Mother,

RUDYARD KIPLING
in NEW ENGLAND

RUDYARD KIPLING
in NEW ENGLAND

By
Howard C. Rice

REPRINTED BY PERMISSION FROM
THE NEW ENGLAND QUARTERLY, IX, 3
(SEPTEMBER, 1936)
WITH CORRECTIONS
AND ADDITIONS

BRATTLEBORO *Stephen Daye Press* VERMONT, 1936

ILLUSTRATIONS

THE TWO ILLUSTRATIONS ARE
FROM ORIGINALS IN THE COLLECTION OF

Mrs. J. H. Soliday

RUDYARD KIPLING
in NEW ENGLAND

Naulakha, at Brattleboro, Vermont

Rudyard Kipling in New England

THE death of Rudyard Kipling has led people to review the details of his astonishing career. Universal renown came to him so early that younger readers of to-day look on him as belonging to a remote generation of "classics." They may have been surprised to learn that he was only seventy at the time of his death. Others have wondered at the fact that the poet of British imperialism and the story-teller of British India married an American wife and once lived in the United States. That *The Jungle Books* were written among the hills of Vermont has seemed not only paradoxical but incredible.

The tradition of visiting English authors and commentators is so well established now that Kipling's visit would call for no more than passing mention if he had come over as a writer in search of material or a lecturer looking for audiences. The facts are quite otherwise: he built his first home in New England, and there he wrote some of his best-known books. Although the circumstances of Kipling's residence in America, as well as "incidents" caused by certain of his remarks, have been recalled recently, few people know, or have cared to inquire how it was that Kipling happened to settle in New

England—what he thought of it, and what New England thought of him.

To understand Kipling's reasons for coming to live in the United States it is necessary to recall the figure of a now-forgotten American writer, Wolcott Balestier, who was born in Rochester, New York, in 1861, but spent much of his childhood in the home of his grandparents, Mr. and Mrs. Joseph Nerée Balestier, near Brattleboro, Vermont. As the name of the family indicates, the Balestiers were not of native stock. Joseph had come to the United States as a child from Martinique in the West Indies. After an active business career in Chicago he retired to a country home which he built near Brattleboro. He had first become acquainted with this region through a visit to the once fashionable Wesselhoeft water-cure. His grandson, Wolcott, began his career as a writer in New York. He was for a time employed in the Astor Library, wrote a life of Blaine for the presidential campaign of 1884, and soon published several novels—among them *Victorious Defeat* and *Benefits Forgot*. In 1888, young Balestier was sent to London as representative and agent for John W. Lovell, a New York publisher. With a flair for business and a gift for making friends, Balestier very soon had a wide acquaintance among English writers and publishers.

He became a partner of the firm of Heinemann and Balestier, among whose activities was the publication of *The English Library,* a series of English and American books designed to compete with the Tauchnitz Edition. In his office in Dean's Yard, Westminster, and in the home which he maintained with his sister, Caroline Starr Balestier, he received in 1889 a young English author who had just returned from India by way of the United States—Rudyard Kipling.

Departmental Ditties and *Plain Tales from the Hills* had already attracted wide attention; other tales of India were being published. This twenty-three-year-old Anglo-Indian journalist had also written for the Indian newspapers, *The Pioneer* and *The Pioneer Mail,* a series of letters describing his discovery of America. These were soon published in a pirated edition under the title of *American Notes,* and later, in an "accurate and authorized edition" as *From Sea to Sea* (1899). The United States was not a wholly strange land to Kipling when he disembarked at San Francisco. Not only had he encountered a wide variety of American travellers along the road from Mandalay to California, but he had read many books by American writers. As the train carried him along the banks of the Sacramento River, all the characters in Bret Harte's stories waved a welcome to him. Farther north, the Columbia seemed to be the Mississippi, and he could almost recognize the reaches down which Huck Finn and Jim had drifted. (When he arrived in the East, he succeeded in obtaining an interview with Mark Twain.) The novels of Henry James had prepared young Ruddy for the American maiden he met in Yellowstone Park, while Louisa Alcott had made him familiar with the "little women" he found in a Pennsylvania town. There were, then, these agreeable discoveries of familiar things, but there were also unpleasant experiences and encounters. It is impossible to talk of Kipling's opinion of the United States during his first visit—he had a wide variety of opinions, ranging from exuberantly youthful enthusiasm to petulant chauvinism. He cursed America magnificently when he found a pirated edition of one of his books (the curse was not included in *From Sea to Sea*!), but he also wrote a "moral treatise" in praise of American girls, and made such statements as this:

Let there be no misunderstanding about the matter. I love this People, and if any contemptuous criticism has to be done, I will do it myself. My heart has gone out to them beyond all other peoples; and for the life of me I cannot tell why. They are bleeding-raw at the edges, almost more conceited than the English, vulgar with a massive vulgarity which is as though the Pyramids were coated with Christmas-cake sugar-work. Cocksure they are, lawless and as casual as they are cocksure; but I love them, and I realised it when I met an Englishman who laughed at them. . . . .[1]

Kipling's heart "went out" to Wolcott Balestier, the young American writer and publisher he met in London. These two collaborated in the writing of *The Naulahka,* published in 1892, a "story of West and East" recounting the search of one Nicholas Tarvin of Topaz, Colorado, for the fabulously beautiful jewel worn by a Hindu maharajah. In 1891, while he was in Dresden in the interests of *The English Library,* Balestier was stricken with typhus, and died there on December 6 shortly before his thirtieth birthday. None was more affected by this tragic news than Rudyard Kipling, who wrote of his friend:

Scarce had he need to cast his pride or slough the dross of earth.
E'en as he trod that day to God, so walked he from his birth—
In simpleness and gentleness and honour and clean mirth.[2]

A few weeks after Wolcott Balestier's death the newspapers announced the engagement of his sister Caroline and friend Rudyard Kipling. Their marriage took place in London in January 1892. It was natural that Mrs. Kipling's thoughts should at such a time turn to her family in America and to the hills where her brother and she had spent much of their childhood together. So, soon after their marriage, the Kiplings set out for the United States on the S. S. Teutonic. Their presence aboard enlivened the crossing for at least one of their world-weary fellow passengers, Henry Adams, who writes in his *Education*:

> Fate was kind on that voyage. Rudyard Kipling, on his wedding trip to America, thanks to the mediation of Henry James, dashed over the passenger his exuberant fountain of gaiety and wit—as though playing a garden hose on a thirsty and faded begonia. Kipling could never know what peace of mind he gave, for he could hardly ever need it himself so much; and yet, in the full delight of his endless fun and variety, one felt the old conundrum repeat itself. Somehow, somewhere, Kipling and the American were not one, but two, and could not be glued together. . . . .

Adams' words, read in the light of Kipling's later experiences, are ominous.

After the briefest of stops in New York the Kiplings turned north, leaving behind them the city "with her roar and rattle, her complex smells, her triply overheated rooms, and much too energetic inhabitants." They arrived in Vermont on the evening of the seventeenth of February, 1892. The thermometer marked thirty below freezing. Kipling caught his breath as he stepped from the train into the midnight air, and then into the waiting sleigh, piled high with blankets and buffalo robes. Snow such as this was a new experience for him— he had previously seen it only from a distance, on the peaks of the Himalayas. He has described in *Letters of Travel* the deep impression made on him by this moonlit sleigh-ride through a snow-covered countryside, "beautiful beyond expression."

The spectacle that greeted him the next morning was no less beautiful: a bright white landscape and sapphire blue sky, such as New England offers in her happier moods. Apparently it was a case of love at first sight, for during this brief February visit the Kiplings purchased a pasture of eleven and one half acres on which to build a home. The lot, which was just over the Brattleboro line in the town of Dummerston, adjoined the farm of Mrs. Kipling's grandparents. That summer, after a trip to Japan, they came back to supervise the building of the house, for which a family friend, Henry Rutgers Marshall, had drawn the plans. During the months that followed, they lived at the neighboring "Bliss Cottage" where, shortly before it was time to move into the new house, their first child was born.

Kipling's father, John Lockwood Kipling, himself an author and artist, visited his son during the latter months of 1892. He, too, watched the construction of the house with the greatest interest. On the mantelpiece in his son's study he inscribed the words, THE NIGHT COMETH WHEN NO MAN CAN WORK, and to the furnishing of this new home he contributed, among other things, India print hangings which are still in place. The gray-shingled house, reminiscent of the bungalows of India, was called "Naulakha," the name of the fabulous Indian jewel in the novel written by Kipling and Wolcott Balestier.

In 1892 the hillside on which Naulakha was built—it has been pointed out that Kipling always spelled the name of his house "Naulakha," and the title of his novel "Naulahka"—was a treeless pasture. To-day the house is scarcely visible from the road, hidden as it is behind trees and shrubs, many of which Kipling planted with his own hands. To a friend who visited the partly constructed house Kipling explained the theory of it. The house was his ship: "The propeller, that is, the material provision of the furnace and kitchen, at the stern, and his own study, opening up on the roomy piazza looking to the south and east, at the bow." The rooms on each of the three floors all face the east, and are entered from long corridors along the western side of the house, where the main entrance is also to be found. To the east of the house green fields slope down to the road, and far off on the horizon is Mount Monadnock, "like a giant thumbnail pointing heavenward." Kipling had a great liking for this mountain, which he called his weather prophet. Many years earlier he had come across this name in a parody of Emerson's style. The word had shuttled in and out of his memory until it had led him to Emerson's poem on the wise old giant "busy with his sky affairs." Then he became acquainted with the mountain itself, and finally gave to one of his own essays the title "In Sight of Monadnock."

Here at Naulakha, in sight of Monadnock, Kipling lived and worked until August, 1896. Although he disliked any unnecessary invasion of his private life, he was the most genial and hospitable of hosts to those whom he accepted as his friends. With one of these, the late Miss Mary R. Cabot, the present writer has had the privilege of many conversations. From such memories and from the record to be found in Kipling's own writings it has been possible to reconstruct this account of the famous author's residence in America. Those who saw him in the village streets recall his impressive

coachman and carriage, or perhaps his own some-
what unprepossessing appearance which sometimes caused him to be mistaken for "some weather-
beaten farmhand, bent from much hoeing on
Vermont hills." But those who made frequent visits
to Naulakha have another picture of the man.
They all recall his captivating conversation, which
embraced everything from remote rajahs of India to English society and American politics. They
remember, too, the keen power of observation in
his eyes which, from behind thick glasses, took in
every part of a scene at a glance, or his amazing
memory, which would revive the details of some
small incident long forgotten by every one else.

Occasionally he would read chapters from some
work in progress; again he would delight his guests
by composing innumerable verses upon some fool-
ish or insignificant remark. With his left hand he
would drum out the metre, while reciting the
verses as rapidly as possible, and sometimes draw
illustrations with his right hand. But no matter
how clever such verses might be, Kipling would
rarely allow any one to write them down and save
them. On Sunday he often spent part of the day
composing hymns, for he disliked going to church,
where he knew he would be stared at. Before he de-
stroyed these verses he would read them to his Mon-

day guests. A small model theatre provided another diversion. In this Kipling would manipulate the entrances and exits of paper figures while discussing his ambition to write a play. He often did write plays for the amusement of his guests—especially successful was a Christmas Eve skit in which each guest played the part of himself.

Not all Kipling's amusements were indoors. With one of his American friends, "a quiet slow-spoken man of the West . . . . who loved the woods for their own sake, and not for the sake of slaughter," he took long walks on snowshoes, learned about the manners and customs of New Englanders at home and along the new railway lines in the Far West, of the animals and birds of the Vermont woods, and the Indian names of mountains and brooks. With another friend he devised a system of snow golf, described as follows:

We played golf over snow two feet deep, upon the crust, cutting holes into the soft snow, and naturally losing the balls, until it occurred to him to ink them red. The first day we experimented with them, we dyed the plain like some football gridiron or Hohenlinden; then we had them painted. The trouble with golfing on the crust was that as the meadow was upon a side hill with gradual slope, a ball went on for ever when once started unless headed off by some kindly stone wall or by one's opponent. It was an easy matter to make a drive of two miles. As spring came little putting greens emerged like oases in the snow, and then we had holes made of empty vegetable cans sunk in the moist soil, round which we would manoeuvre in rubber boots. For a touch of courtesy I recall his intentional miss of a hole one inch away, throwing the victory to me, who was a stroke and five yards behind him. Retiring from outdoor sports, we would repair to the library for tea and talk.[3]

There were no visitors at Naulakha before lunch. In the library, at the bow of his "ship," Kipling worked every morning from nine until one. To enter this room it was necessary to pass through a smaller one, "the dragon's chamber," where Mrs. Kipling sat with her sewing. No one resented more fiercely than she any intrusion or interruption of her husband's working hours. The amount of work accomplished here in the study at Naulakha is impressive. Among the books completed or written during the years 1892-1896 were: the two *Jungle Books,* some of the short stories included in *The Day's Work,* many of the poems in *The Seven Seas,* and *Captains Courageous. The Jungle Books* must have been already formulated in Kipling's imagination, if not actually written down, at the time of his arrival in Vermont. At a Thanksgiving dinner in the home of a friend, he described for the benefit of the children present, the doings

NAULAKHA.
BRATTLEBORO
VERMONT.

To Messrs   Aug: 25 · 1895.

Farquhar & Co.

Gentlemen:

I ordered from you this Spring,
some four and twenty H.P. roses,
hollyhocks; peonies, zinnias asters and
one or two other plants for my garden.
I think it only fair to let you know
that everything you sent was both
thoroughly good of its kind and
entirely satisfactory in growth. I lost only
two of the H.P's; the others blooming
beautifully. The hollyhocks are now
over four foot high, loaded with blossom
and both zinnias and marigolds
(particularly the frilled 'African'
variety) as fine as could be desired.
In fact the success of the garden this
year is in large measure due to
your supplies.
I wish now that your firm would
send me (by mail or express as
seems best) one hundred and fifty
good strawberry plants of a variety
sufficiently hardy to endure our
Vermont winters. I cannot at this
present moment set hands on your
catalogue and so must trust to your
judgment which I am sure will
be correct. I should prefer layered

plants if possible in order to get better
fruit next spring.

I should also be obliged if you would
send me your catalogue as soon as
possible, as I wish to grow some Tea roses &c
for indoor blooming this winter.

If you will let me know cost of plants
& expressage I will forward cheque.

Yours faithfully
Rudyard Kipling

of the troops of monkeys he had known in India. The description made a vivid impression upon the adults as well as upon the children, although they probably did not then realize that the doings of the Bandar-Log were soon to command the attention of an audience as wide as the world. There is an interesting story connected with the manuscript of the first draft of "Mowgli's Brothers." In February, 1893, Kipling gave this to Miss Susan Bishop, the nurse who had cared for Mrs. Kipling and the infant daughter born in the late autumn of 1892. He told the nurse that she was to sell it if she were ever hard up. She did so some years later, and the manuscript found its way eventually into the hands of the late William M. Carpenter, a collector of Kipling.

Although *The Jungle Books* were inspired by much earlier experiences, the germ of another book, *Captains Courageous: A Story of the Grand Banks,* seems to have been planted in Kipling's mind at Naulakha. Dr. James Conland, the family physician, who had shipped as a sailor in his boyhood, was a frequent visitor. Kipling often listened to his stories of adventures aboard fishing vessels, coasters, and East India traders; later he made a trip to Gloucester in the company of Dr. Conland and other friends. The manuscript of *Captains*

21

Courageous, which was given to Dr. Conland, later came into the possession of the Morgan Library.[4] In the printed volume one can still read the dedication to this friend, with these verses by Longfellow:

> I ploughed the land with horses,
>   But my heart was ill at ease,
> For the old sea-faring men
> Came to me now and then,
>   With their sagas of the seas.

During this period Kipling's fame and the demand for his work were constantly growing. He succeeded in 1895 in having a private post-office established at a cross-roads near his home, called "Waite" after the name of the postmistress, Miss Anna F. Waite. He even hoped for a private railroad station. One of Kipling's friends related the following story concerning the popularity of his work: Kipling once received from Mr. Bok, the editor of the *Ladies' Home Journal,* a request to write a story for that periodical, a magazine for which he had a particular dislike. Thinking to outwit Bok, Kipling replied in the affirmative but deliberately set an exhorbitant sum as his price. To his astonishment, the offer was immediately accepted; so he proceeded to submit the manuscript of "William the Conqueror." A few days later there arrived a letter from Bok, who requested that other beverages be substituted for the whiskey and champagne mentioned in the story, because it was against the principles of the *Ladies' Home Journal* to mention the use of intoxicating liquors. Kipling replied that such a substitution was impossible, and that the story must be published as written or not at all. Bok yielded, and Kipling always liked to tell his friends how he had forced the *Ladies' Home Journal* to print the name of an alcoholic beverage.[5]

Occasional traces of Kipling's New England experiences are to be found in his better known works. For example, there is the Whale in the *Just So Stories* who "opened his mouth wide and wide and wide, and said, 'Change here for Winchester, Ashuelot, Nashua, Keene, and stations on the *Fitch*burg Road'; and just as he said 'Fitch' the Mariner walked out of his mouth. . . . ." And there are the verses,

Robin down the logging-road whistles, "Come to me,"
Spring has found the maple-grove, the sap is running
     free. . . . .

Diligent Kipling admirers have even dug up uncollected bits of Kiplingiana-Americana such as,

"How Breitmann Became President on the Bicy-
cle Ticket."[6] But it is a few fugitive essays, later
brought together with others and published in
1920 under the title *Letters of Travel,* that record
Kipling's mature impressions of the American
scene. The popular notion that Kipling strongly
disliked America is not borne out by a careful read-
ing of such essays as those entitled "In Sight of
Monadnock,"[7] "On One Side Only" and "Leaves
from a Winter Note-Book." It would be hard to
find, even among American writers, any more
keenly observant and appreciative pages on a New
England winter: the strength of a great blizzard,
the "splendid jewellery" of the ice-storm, the "blue,
breathless" days, the Japanese landscapes in black
and white. Kipling was aware, too, of the terror and
solitude of such a season, breeding dreams, visions,
hatred, and fear in the minds of lonely, brooding
men and women. He delighted in the late but mi-
raculous spring, taking note of the "first blood-root
. . . between the patches of April snow"—"green
against the draggled drift, faint and frail and first"—
and the other wild flowers in their season. He cele-
brated the first mayflower in one of his poems, and
once declared to a friend that he would never think
of leaving Naulakha while the wood-anemones
were in bloom. The "flaming blood-red maples"

won his admiration in autumn; while during his first summer in Vermont he decided that the New England summer had creole blood in her veins!

It is not surprising to find that a man who described with such skill the animals of the East should also observe the animals of the West: the woodchuck down in the field, the red squirrels among the beeches and hickories, and the "partridges" eating the checkerberries on the outskirts of the wood. He learned to recognize the tracks of fox and deer in the snow, and the sorrowful cry of "brer coon" at night. Although there is but a casual mention of these animals in his writing, Kipling did make at least one attempt to build a story around his new acquaintances: "A Walking Delegate," the chief characters of which are Vermont horses. One can still see in Kipling's study at Naulakha plaster casts of Bagheera and Grey Brother which were given him by Joel Chandler Harris. The Uncle Remus characters were old friends of his, and he was struck by the fact that he could find a prototype for many of them in the folklore of India. In a letter to Harris who had reviewed *The Second Jungle Book,* Kipling wrote:

I wonder if you could realize how "Uncle Remus," his sayings, and the sayings of the noble beasties ran like wild fire through an English public school when I was about fifteen. We used to go to battle (with boots and bolsters and such-like) against those whom we did not love, to the tune of *Ty-yi-tungalee: I eat um pea, I pick um pea,* etc., and I remember the bodily bearing into a furze-bush of a young fag solely because his nickname had been "Rabbit" before the tales invaded the school and—well, we assumed that he ought to have been "bawn and bred in a briar-patch," and gorse was the most efficient substitute. And six years ago in India, meeting an old school-mate of those days, we found ourselves quoting whole pages of "Uncle Remus" that had got mixed in with the fabric of the old school life. . . . .[8]

It is amusing to imagine that Brer Rabbit and Rikki-tikki-tavi and the Elephant's Child joined hands, in Kipling's mind at least—belying his own famous words about East and West.

Kipling's interest was not confined to the American landscape, to plants and animals; it extended to the inhabitants of the country about his home. "The long, unhurried drawl of Vermont" was a source of constant wonder to him. He thought that New England dialect, although supposedly written in English and its type, might just as well be printed in Swedish or Russian! But he liked these people: "Unhandy men to cross in their ways, set, silent, indirect in speech, and as impenetrable as that other Eastern farmer who is the bedrock of another land." They did not often appear in the papers; they told very little in the outsider's estimate of America, and yet several millions of these people *were* Americans. Kipling observed the social transformations which were taking place in this region. He was acquainted with the deserted farms twenty or thirty miles across the hills on the way to the Green Mountains, "started in a lean land, held fiercely as long as there was any one to work them, and then left on the hill-sides." He knew that the West and the cities were draining this country of its inhabitants—farmers who a generation earlier had made their own clothes, soap, candles, and food, but who were now buying shop-made clothes, patent soaps and kerosene. Nothing amused him more than the race of itinerant peddlers and wandering quacks who annually invaded the region, hawking their wares from farm to farm: huge red-and-gilt biographies of Presidents, twenty-pound family Bibles, genuine steel engravings, patent electric pills, seeds, pins, and flavoring-extracts! About one of these, a florist's representative peddling seeds, who had come "to swindle every citizen from Keene to Lake Champlain," Kipling wrote a poem in 1893—"Pan in Vermont."[9]

There is, then, plenty of evidence to show that Kipling appreciated, and even loved, many of the things he found in America. But it would be a mistake to think that this appreciation and affection included all Americans and all things American. There were many things he did not like, and the bluntness with which he stated his opinions often stirred resentment. He had little sympathy for the summer boarders, who came from the Cities of the Plain, faithfully dragging their telephones and telegraphs after them, panting to do things, talking of "getting there" and "being left." The droves of women with their kodaks, their Nerves, and their passion for stripping the bark off white birches to make blue-ribboned waste-paper baskets especially annoyed him. This antipathy dated back to his tour through Yellowstone Park in 1889. He spoke scathingly of their "Gospel of Rush," and remarked that they would return "partially civilised, soon to be resavaged by the clash of a thousand wars whose echo does not reach here."

Kipling had little good to say of New York City. He inveighed against its lawlessness, its squalid barbarism, its reckless extravagance, its disregard for human life, its shiftlessness, and its corruption. All these unflattering remarks, including the reference to "the long, narrow pig-trough" are preserved for the curious to read in the essay, "Across a Continent." Nor did Kipling wholly overcome his mistrust of Main Street, the term he used to describe the small town near his residence. To him it seemed that the inhabitants lived on terms of "terrifying intimacy." He noticed that although Main Street had little to do with strangers like himself, Main Street knew everything—and much more —that went on among them. Their clothing, their cattle, the manners of their children, their bearing towards servants—all such matters and many more were reported and discussed. Although he complained that the native wisdom of Vermont was not always equal to the task of grasping the problems of others with delicacy—that its mistakes were sometimes pathetic—he philosophically concluded that towns of a certain size were more or less similar the whole world over.

Kipling, like many other English visitors to the United States before and since, resented what he termed Yankee curiosity—what the Yankees themselves doubtless thought was nothing more than being friendly or neighborly. He at one time devised an ingenious scheme for discouraging autograph-seekers, informing each applicant by a printed card that he would send his signature when the correspondent had contributed two dollars and a half to the Tribune Fresh Air Fund. Over two hundred contributions to the Fund are said to have been made as a result! But American reporters were his especial bugbear. He had not forgotten those who welcomed him at San Francisco when he first visited the United States in 1889. Many stories are told of his studied attempts to evade their persistent efforts to penetrate into his retreat at Naulakha. Such annoyances colored Kipling's judgments of America and often led him to make those sweeping statements which were quoted widely, and to his disadvantage. A small incident or remark would, according to his friends, often distort his whole view of a subject. These same friends knew better than any one that Kipling remained an Englishman at heart, an Englishman whose patriotism had been sharpened and accentuated by long absence from Great Britain. He could rarely see the gleam of idealism which lay beneath America's commercialism and desire for wealth. With one of his Vermont friends Kipling used to discuss "The Great American Novel" and his own ambition to write it; but this friend could only smile to herself, for she realized that, in spite of his genius, he lacked the necessary understanding of America to do this. It was Henry Adams' "old conundrum." In 1894, however, he made his most serious attempt to define the essence of America in the poem, "The American Spirit Speaks," with its well-known lines,

> The cynic devil in his blood
> That bids him mock his hurrying soul,
> That bids him flout the Law he makes,
> That bids him make the Law he flouts.

Kipling accused Americans of a "savage paro-chial pride that squeals under a steady stare or a pointed finger," and yet he himself fiercely resented any criticism of British policy. During his residence in America the dispute between Great Britain and the United States over the boundary of Venezuela called forth, in a certain section of the American press, that latent Anglophobia which bursts out time and again—sometimes on the slightest pretext. As he read such articles he would, according to a friend, "smile a quiet smile" and make "mental comparison of American and English navies." To another friend he wrote:

This damned Venezuela rot has made me sick to my heart. It may be fine and picturesque and patriotic and all the rest of it, but it has done America a damage it will take her fifty years to recover from, in the eyes of the civilized world.[10]

Once when a luncheon guest at Naulakha replied rather flippantly to some remark on the trouble in Venezuela, Kipling asked her with some ve-hemence if she realized that "The Great White

31

Squadron" could wipe out the cities on the Atlantic coast of her country within a few days. When the lady acknowledged that she did not and questioned the truth of the supposition, her host became so angry that he got up and left the table. Such touchiness is not surprising to those who recall the glorification of the Empire which came from his pen in the next few years, combined with bitter attacks on opponents at home and abroad who dared to question his peculiar brand of imperialism.

Kipling's plans for Naulakha had every evidence of permanence. On various occasions both he and his wife expressed the opinion that the conditions there were ideal for his creative work. The achievements of these years would seem to confirm the statements. While it is clear that Kipling's adaptation to American ways was never complete, and that his patriotic feelings were stirred by talk of "hereditary foes," yet it is doubtful if these factors alone would have led him to leave Vermont had not an unpleasant quarrel crystallized latent resentment. A discussion with a near relative over a boundary line led to an altercation and blustering threats. The case got into court; so what might have remained a row in the family became the property of the public. To have private affairs discussed in Main Street was bad enough, but the presence of reporters from the metropolitan dailies was insufferable to a man of Kipling's sensitiveness. The calm of Naulakha and the peace of his own mind were completely shattered. In August, 1896, he left Vermont and returned to England, there to make his home.

In 1899 Kipling made his last visit to the United States. Not only was he critically ill in New York, but his eldest child, Josephine, died at the same time. In spite of painful associations, however, Kipling must have preserved many pleasant memories of the four years during which he lived in Vermont. At a later date he wrote to a friend there that his wife and he were crouched over an inadequate fire aching with the English cold and longing for Naulakha. The dwelling still stands—firmly anchored to its hillside, a reminder that Kipling once made that land his home.

In 1922, when the newspapers were heatedly discussing some disparaging remarks which Kipling made on America's rôle in the war, a New York columnist protested: "What difference does it make if he is an insufferable Tory? He wrote *The Jungle Book*. Has everybody forgotten that?" A similar question might well be asked here. What difference do all these details of his life in New England make? The real account of Kipling in

America is not that of a mortal man who quarrelled over a patch of land with a neighbor—but rather the history of Mowgli, of Kim, of Rikki-tikki, of the Cat that Walked by Himself, and of all their tribe, in the minds and the hearts of Americans. But that, to use Kipling's own phrase, "is another story."

Notes

NOTES

[1] *From Sea to Sea,* XXXIII.

[2] Dedication *To Wolcott Balestier, Ballads and Barrack-Room Ballads,* 1892.

[3] Reverend C. O. Day, "Rudyard Kipling As Seen in His Vermont Home" (1899), reprinted in Mary R. Cabot, *Annals of Brattleboro* (Brattleboro, Vermont, 1922). Miss Cabot's two-volume work contains other valuable information which has been used in this article. Some additional material is to be found in Charles Crane, *Pendrift* (Brattleboro, 1931).

[4] The opening passage of the manuscript is reproduced in facsimile in *The Hartford Courant,* January 19, 1936. The original title was "Harvey Cheyne-Banker."

[5] Bok's version of the story will be found in his *The Americanization of Edward Bok* (New York, 1920), pp. 219-220. E. A. Ballard, to whom the Kipling-Bok correspondence "was once offered," also recounts the incident in his *Catalogue . . . . of my Kipling Collection* (Philadelphia, privately printed, 1935).

[6] Published in *The New York World,* April 26, 1896. Described in Lloyd H. Chandler, *A Summary of the Work of Rudyard Kipling* (N. Y., Grolier Club, 1930), p. 118.

[7] This letter was first printed in *The Times* (London) and *The Sun* (New York), April 1892, in *The Civil & Military Gazette,* May 1892, and later in *The Springfield Republican*. It first appeared in book form in a commercial compilation entitled *Picturesque Brattleboro,* Reverend Frank T. Pomeroy, Editor, (Northampton, Mass., 1894). A comparison of this version with the earlier one shows that many sentences, and even whole paragraphs, were omitted. The nature of these omissions seems to indicate that either Kipling himself, or perhaps the cautious editor, desired to spare the susceptibilities of prospective purchasers of *Picturesque Brattleboro.* This expurgated version of "In Sight of Monadnock" was also reprinted in *The Vermonter* for April, 1899. Finally, there was a separate reprint of the essay by the Cornhill Press, Boston, 1904, and even a reprint falsely dated 1894, about 1918!

This information is to be found in Mrs. F. V. Livingston's *Bibliography of the Works of Rudyard Kipling* (New York, 1927), without which guide no amateur should venture into the jungle of Kipling bibliography.

[8] Letter written from Waite, Vermont, December 6, 1895, published in Julia C. Harris, *The Life and Letters of Joel Chandler Harris* (Boston & New York, 1918), pp. 332-334.

[9] This poem was first published in *Country Life in America,* December 1902. The same year a few copies in

pamphlet form were issued in London for copyright pur-
poses—another rare collector's item!

[10] In a letter dated Waite, January 10, 1896, to W. Hal-
lett Phillips. Quoted in book and autograph catalogue of
Alwin J. Scheuer, New York (catalogue no. 6, 1931, item
2548).